Concise Guide
to
SPORTS-CARS

Text by
Franco Mazza

THE SPORTS CAR

A DRIVE THROUGH THE PAST

We shall begin our journey through the world of motor cars by trying to recreate something of the atmosphere and excitement of the race itself. The history of racing cars should not be a mere survey of their technical development and design. It should capture the thrill of the race track, the audacity and daring of the drivers and their relationship with an enthusiastic public. For this reason we have gathered together some of the most interesting and representative articles from contemporary magazines and newspapers. Apart from recreating the atmosphere of the times, they also show how close the contact was between the trial of particular technical features in racing and their use in the ordinary production car. Here is a significant passage from the Italian touring Club magazine of 1914:

*SIZAIRE-NAUDIN,
two-seater
racer, 1908.
One vertical
cylinder of 1490
cc., 100 km per
hour.
The vehicle had
great racing
success
amongst the
vehicles of its
times. Note
the independent
front wheels.*

*Right:
a prototype of a
sports car
steering-wheel.*

Dufaux, two-seater racer, 1904. Eight cylinders, 12761 cc., 80 hp, 140 km/h. This powerful racing-car participated in the eliminations for the Gordon Bennet Cup in 1904.

"Everyone interested in motor cars will certainly have noticed the great victory achieved with Continental tyres at the A.C.F. Gran Prix in Lyon last July. Lautnschlager, Wagner and Salzer driving Mercedes equipped with Continental tyres came in

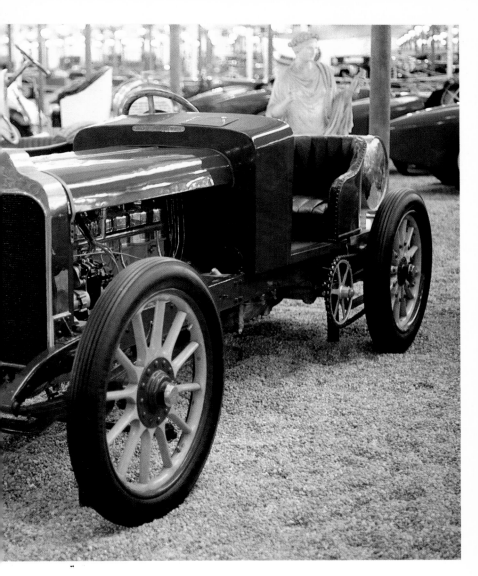

first, second and third. None of them suffered the
least trouble with their tyres, despite the difficulty
of the terrain (in a few places the ruts were a metre
deep) and the many bends taken at high speed
which put the tyres under considerable strain.

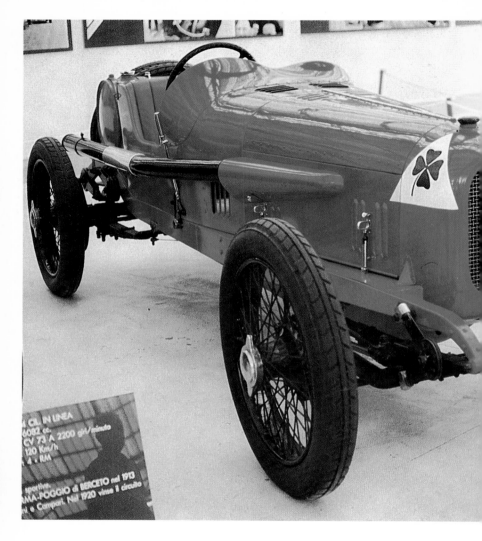

Salzer made the fastest lap, reaching 123 km per hour for 15 out of the 20 laps of the circuit and came in with the best time. All this shows much better than words how good Continental tyres are and provides the best recommendation for this make."

Magazines like that of the Italian Touring Club

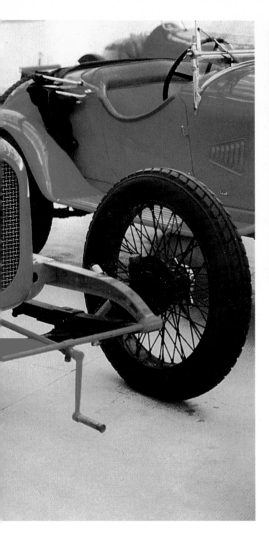

*ALFA RL, TARGA FLORIO, 1923.
Six cylinders, 3 litres, valves in
the head. This vehicle repesents
the first masterpiece of the Arese
company.*

often carried articles about motor cars and no doubt
helped these new machines to become popular
among the general public. In the same magazine in
April 1914 there appeared the following article en-
titled *The Modern Motor Car*:

"This year the Aquila Italiana has once more dis-
tinguished itself in the 5000 kilometre Tour de

BUGATTI 32 TANK, two-seater racer, 1923. Eight cylinders, 1991 cc., 190 km/h. Bugatti, an aviation enthusiast, gave this vehicle the shape of an aeroplane-wing cross-section.

France. The race was run in terrible conditions for the competitors and only one third managed to complete the course. The three Aquilas taking part not only finished, but performed so well as to attract the attention of the *Miral dell'Auto* which wrote: 'The Tour de France will give this Italian make its chance to demonstrate how well its cars are made... in all the tests we see these cars per-

forming well. Already a top make in Italy, I reckon the firm will soon establish a reputation for itself in France too.'" And later on: "The Beria 4-Cylinder sports car is an adorable machine and the Tour de France will give it a chance to show off what it can do."

In the magazine *Motor Italia* of June 1934, we have found the following description of the "Alfa-

Romeo that won on the Avus Circuit."

"The aerodynamic Alfa-Romeo in which Guy Moll won the Avus race on May 27, is the first Italian racing car to illustrate a new concept in streamling. For the design of the bodywork, the

Alfa 6C 1750 Gran Sport, 1930.
This car represents the height of style and technology of its times and is one of the most famous Alfas. It took part in a large number of races, among which the epic duel of Varzi and Nuvolari in the Thousand Miles.

Scuderia Ferrari had the bright idea of commissioning a well known aviation engineer, Pallavicino. He worked first for Breda in Milan and is currently director of the Caproni Workshop in Ponte San Pietro. Pallavicino has designed

some of our fastest aeroplanes. His design for the Alfa is very original, the cross-section of which is in the shape of a person sitting at the driving wheel. The headrest extends along the back and forms a sort of tail fin. The pointed tails behind the wheels tone down a bit the windswept effect of the

ALFA 12C,
4064 cc, 1936.
This is the first 12-cylinder
engine made by the Arese
makers. This vehicle won the
Vanderbilt Cup in 1936.

vehicle, but even the front part of the chassis with its spring suspension has been streamlined. Despite its extra weight in comparison to the normal single seater Alfa-Romeo, on test runs along the Milan-Lakes motorway the car accelerated well. The engine was of the usual 8 cylinder type, 2905 cc, giv-

Großer Preis von Deutschland
auf dem Nürburgring 25.Juli 1937 Beginn 11 Uhr

*Ettore Bugatti,
born in Milan but French by
adoption,built the most important
vehicles of the 20's and 30's in his
Molsheim factory in Alsace. All the
versions had speed as one of their
main prerequisites. On this page
one example of many displayed at
the Mulhouse Museum.*

ing 260 HP at 5400 revs per minute, or about 90 HP per litre."

After the war motor racing began again. It was at this time that the Ferrari legend really started. An article by F. Fasole describes a visit to Maranello.

"The 'temple of speed' is a new and simply laid out plant. In Enzo Ferrari's spacious office, for ex-

ample, the walls are bare of pictures or photo-
graphs and the room is devoid of decoration.
Perhaps there is a hidden charm behind this clean
austerity. That is only to be expected when you
hear the ideas and instructions expounded by him,
Enzo Ferrari, or "Sir" as everyone calls him. (This
is a title of which he can be proud and which he

earned as an ace of the track at the age of 25 when
he spectacularly won on the circuit at Pescara.)
Incisive and colourful in conversation, he says:
'There are big firms where what you notice is the

ALFA SINGLE-SEATER AERODYNAMIC TYPE B, 1934.
This car, with bodywork designed by the engineer Pallavicino, won the Avus Gran Prix in 1934.
Those who studied aerodynamics achieved very good results in the 1930's, also from a formal point of view.

elegant marble of the offices and buildings, but if you look beyond the appearances there's nothing else there. The strength of a company is not in its buildings but in the men who work inside them.'"

INVICTA SPORT, 4500 CC, LOW CHASSIS, 1930. This English company made up for its lack of aerodynamics by using more cylinders.

The Thousand Miles Race has an American version in the Carrera Panamerica. In November 1951 the New York Times correspondent, R. Georges, described the victory of Taruffi-Chinetti, who was driving a Ferrari, in this way:

"Against the two Ferraris our cars had no chances of winning. In fact, if the Italians hadn't been held

up by tyre trouble early on, the race would have been wound up from the beginning. Our tendency to obtain power through big cylindered and consequently heavy machines is now out of date. Against the Ferrari's 1200 kilos, producing 160 horse power with only 2560 cc, our best car, the Chrysler Saratoga, with more than double the

During the 30's th
small ridges on th
views - they are sp

omobile faced the problems of lightness and aerodynamics. The MG has hints of
dguards and on the streamlining of the bodywork. Here shown are three MG front
cars and clearly aggressive.

Ferrari's cubic capacity produced 180 horse power and weighed a colossal 2200 kilos. As for stability and braking, the Italians were so superior that these two basic factors won them the race. If on the last laps we were able to win back a few seconds, this

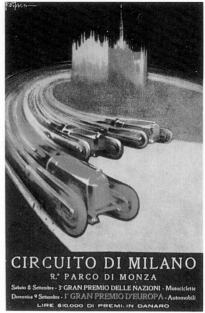

CIRCUITO DI MILANO
R.° PARCO DI MONZA
Sabato 8 Settembre · 3° GRAN PREMIO DELLE NAZIONI · Motociclette
Domenica 9 Settembre · I° GRAN PREMIO D'EUROPA · Automobili
LIRE 610.000 DI PREMI IN DANARO

ALFA ROMEO
COUPE TOURING 8C 2900 B.
An in-depth study of bodywork
shape united with the technical
characteristics of an extremely
advanced engine, together with
fewer cylinders, give particularly
brilliant results. The Alfa engine
is well-fed with two compressors
and is derived from that of the
single-seater type B, of 1934.

was only because the Ferraris already had the race in hand and didn't need to force themselves... What else can I say? The best drivers won with the best cars."

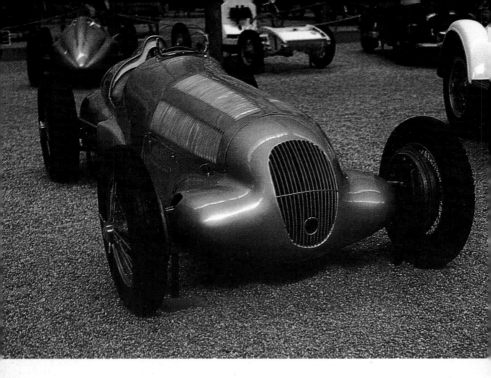

MERCEDES W 125 GRANDPRIX SINGLE-SEATER RACER, 1937. Eight cylinders, 5660 cc; with compressor, 600 hp, 320 km/h. The vehicle that dominated the 1937 season, winning seven out of eleven Grand Prix, with Caracciola, Von Brauchtsh and Lang.

IN RECENT YEARS THE RANGE OF SPORTS CARS HAS CONSIDERABLY INCREASED.
FROM "THE WORLD'S GREAT MAKES", WE DESCRIBE THREE CARS THAT HAVE HELPED TO FORM MOTOR RACING HISTORY AND WHICH ARE STILL VERY MUCH "ON THE TRACK" TODAY.
ELEGANCE AND SPEED HAD ALWAYS BEEN THE MAIN FEATURES OF JAGUAR, AND IT WAS THESE TWO QUALITIES THAT LED TO THE RESOUNDING SUCCESS OF THE CAR WHICH JAGUAR BROUGHT OUT IN 1961.

It was a car which made history, which formed a part of the fabulous sixties. Its soft and sensual lines belong with the memories we have of the Beatles, the mini-skirt of Mary Quant and long hair. These were all English products, from the swinging London of the sixties. And it too was

English: the sensational E-Type Jaguar of 1961.

When it came onto the market it was a shock, partly because the price was much lower than the other sports cars which were then available, cars which only the chosen few could afford. The E-Type matched them for performance and proved it in official races. Besides all this, the car had fabulous charm.

Jaguar needed a car like this to re-launch the firm at the beginning of the sixties. The XK Series, which had achieved great success in 1948,

MERCEDES 300 SLR TWO-SEATER RACER, 1955. Eight cylinders, 2982 cc., 300 hp, 300 km/h. This vehicle was the last to race before the Stoccarda firm's withdrawal from racing.

had to be renewed. A few improvements, such as the addition of disc brakes and a restyling of the bodywork, had given the old hero a new lease of life, but nothing now could disguise its age.

In the meantime Jaguar had made a name for it-

self internationally, achieving legendary victories on the race tracks of the world, especially the Le Mans 24 hour race. The father of the E-Type Jaguar was a man called Malcolm Sayer. He was something of a genius and his ideas were way

The prestigious coat-of-arms of the English BENTLEY, on a luxurious vehicle from the 1930's.

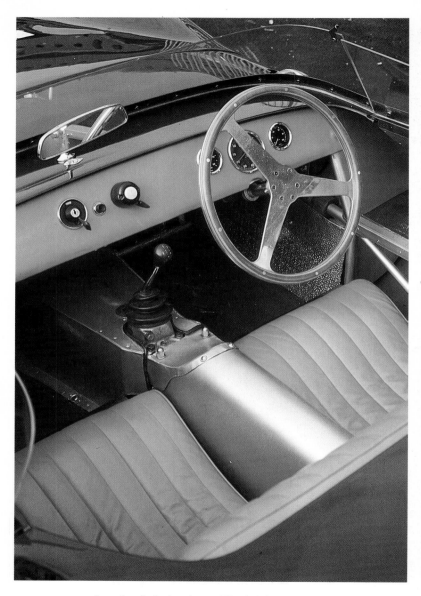

ahead of their time. He had grown up in the air-
craft industry, and this had taught him the impor-
tance of aerodynamics. He designed the body-

The seating-space of the sports vehicle must be spartan, and that of the single-seater virtually inaccessible. In this way the contact between driver and machine is total.

work for the very successful C-Type, which had to preserve a family resemblance with the XK 120. The success of that model convinced the

This BMW with very pleasing lines was built in Turin for the first Thousand Miles race after the war.

Opposite page: Two different kinds of seating-spaces.

Jaguar directors to give him carte blanche for the design of the car that would replace it on the market.

In 1953, Sayer designed a prototype that was incredibly like the car that would eventually be produced eight years later. Working closely with his boss, chief engineer Bill Heynes, Sayer began with a monocoque body, the style of which owed something to the Alfa Romeo Disco Volante. It was from this prototype that the legendary D-Type was developed. Equipped with big, powerful engines and a superbly efficient aerodynamic body, the car beat the Ferrari in many races.

The E-Type Jaguar was launched at the Geneva

Motor Show in March 1961 and received an enthusiastic welcome. Numerous cinema stars
rushed to place their orders. The two cars made
available to the press for trials were assailed by
masses of people who forged press cards in order
to take the car out for a run.

In April four cars were on show at the Jaguar

OSCA 1500
SIMPSON SPECIAL, 1965.
Record-winning cars represent a special chapter in the sports car world. On this page a fascinating Italian product.

Previous page:
the sports JAGUAR C 1953, with an engine of 3442 cubic centimetres.

stand at the New York Motor Show. The stand was besieged by an enthusiastic crowd. The E-Type Jaguar was the unrivalled star of the whole show.

The orders immediately rolled in, especially from the United States, traditionally a large market for Jaguar.

The most begrudging critics said that the car had caught the public's eye only because of its futuristic look and that there was nothing of substance behind it. They were immediately proved wrong. Graham Hill drove one to victory against Ferraris and Aston Martins on the car's first race.

FERRARI.
The Italian style makes an impact after the 2nd World War with its rounded, clean lines, that are apparently simple, but exactly because of this we see they result from a great feat of design.

WHEN IT FIRST CAME OUT, THIRTY YEARS AGO, IT WAS A VERY FAST CAR, BUT IT HAD POOR ROAD HOLDING BECAUSE OF ITS REAR ENGINE. BUT THEN...

The Porsche Turbo has a first-class pedigree, but what kind of car is it? Curiously old-fashioned in

certain respects, it is quite the opposite of its main rivals like the Ferrari Testarossa, the Lamborghini Diablo and even the Chevrolet Corvette ZR-1.

The German firm can never get rid of the fact that the basic design goes back 25 years or so, despite the appearance of re-vamped models in 1988 and 1991. Even the latest model has a narrow, old fashioned interior, the windscreen is more upright than those you generally see today, and the dashboard and instrument panel (very attractive once upon a time) now appears confusing and difficult to read. This is inevitably the first discouraging reaction of someone who may be thinking of paying out the thousands of pounds that the car costs. But in the end patience has its reward. It is sufficient to hear the firm thud when the door closes, to smell the leather seat coverings, to shift the gears and ap-

FERRARI 212 F2 SINGLE-SEATER, 1950.

FERRARI 500/635 F2 SINGLE-SEATER, 1950.

STANGUELLINI JUNIOR 1100 CC, 1958.

Also in the single-seater vehicles the Italian style is composed of simple and well-balanced lines.

preciate one of the most precise mechanisms ever produced by a sports car manufacturer.

The new body, which is a modified version of the highly developed body used on the 911 Carrera 2, offers a number of immediately obvious advantag-

MASERATI 200 SI.
In the Italian racing world, not only Ferrari exists. There are many worthy car builders who brighten racing up in all fields and at all levels of power.

es. Extra space had been created by the shifting forwards of the 13 litre oil sump to the gear-box. This has made it possible to fit an exhaust unit with a three-way catalytic converter.

Inevitably, the Turbo has become 10% heavier as

a result, weighing 1460 kg, although this is com-
pensated for by an increase in horsepower from
300 to 320 HP. Versions fitted with a catalytic con-

The driver's space will become increasingly spartan, with the steering-wheel and instruments reduced to their absolute minimum.

verter gain even more, up to 315 HP from a previous 285 HP. All this makes the Turbo a much faster car than before.

Polyurethane sections front and back have improved the aerodynamic look of the Turbo and given it a family resemblance to the 928 S4 and the four-cylinder 968. The wheels are now 17 inches in diameter and are fitted with classic style rims.

When circumstances allow, it is fascinating to see how fast the speedometer needle moves, transforming this luxury cruising car into a powerful

FERRARI VIGNALE.

JAGUAR D TYPE.

The rear of the sports car is often as fascinating as the front, which evokes the power of the engine, the rear evoking the aerodynamic aspects.

thoroughbred racer.

When a four-speed gear-change was all you could get, a virtue was made of a necessity. "The gear ratio is such that you don't have to change very often... The introduction of five gears now appears like a gift from heaven, reducing the loss of revs when changing gears and heightening the sportive quality of the Turbo."

The other traditional faults of the 911 Turbo have

COSWORTH ENGINE.

FORD ENGINE.

From the 1960's the English revolutionised the character of racing-cars with rear engines, but above all with the general structure of the car.

been reduced or else eliminated today. It is easier to handle and safer while giving the same top quality performance. The Turbo is certainly more even-tempered than its Italian rivals.

WHAT DOES IT TAKE TO TRANSFORM A GREAT NA-ME IN AMERICAN SPORTS CARS INTO AN AUTHENTIC

Ferrari TR 58 Testa Rossa, 1958. Bodywork of exceptional design, mounted on engines made to win and build up the Ferrari myth.

SUPERCAR?
GENERAL MOTORS WENT TO LOTUS FOR ITS V8 ALUMINIUM ENGINE WHICH DELIVERS 375 HP. AND FOR THE REST...

The Corvette has always been the most representative of American sports cars right since its first

appearance in 1953. It was, and still is, the only true two-seater American sports car, but it is also something more. All the technical innovations to have appeared on American cars were first tried out on the Corvette. In the mid-sixties, when all other American cars still had rigid rear suspension

NEWS OF THE WORLD

SPONSOR THE
27th R.A.C.
TOURIST TROPHY RACE
AND THE B.A.R.C. FORMULA JUNIOR CHAMPIONSHIP
GOODWOOD
NEAR CHICHESTER, SUSSEX

SATURDAY, 18th AUGUST, 1962
Programme Starts 12 noon
PUBLIC ENCLOSURES 10/- (CHILDREN 5/-)
CAR PARKS 10/- and 5/-
Racing organised by the British Automobile Racing Club
Advance Bookings: 18 SOUTH STREET, LONDON, W.1.

FERRARI 156 F1 SINGLE-SEATER
GRAN PREMIO, 1963.
The English school influences
Ferrari too.

and drum brakes, the Corvette had disc brakes and totally independent suspension. And yet the Corvette was not without its critics, who, with some reason, said it was too big and heavy and was badly made.

The truth is that Chevrolet had become compla-

Lotus MIC 25, 1962.

cent in its success and had let the Corvette grow old. At the beginning of the eighties, ordinary saloon models could easily leave the Corvette behind. Chevrolet managers finally realised that the time had come to face up to the problem of renewing the model, which no longer lived up to its

name.

Until then General Motors had been accused of showing little imagination, of employing outdated techniques and not guaranteeing high standards of quality. The firm had been able to dominate the market mainly because of the lack of a real com-

petitor. But during the eighties Ford began to sur-
pass GM in terms of technology and style. It was
then that GM's difficulties really began.

The firm had to change its image, start using the

latest technology, build new engines and create a new style. The Corvette was to be the mainstay of this operation. The aim was particularly ambitious. The ZR-1 would quite simply have to be the fastest production car in the world, but at the same time it would have to maintain the handling standards of the old Corvette L98, and keep within the required levels of consumption to avoid the taxes on gas guzzling machines.

The engine was designed by Lotus and built by Mercury Marine in Stillwater, Oklahoma. General Motors wanted the very best quality, and the presentation of the ZR-1 was put off several times until the firm could be really sure that the LTS engine was reliable.

The target of 400 HP was not quite reached. The V8 engine produced 375 HP at 5800 rpm. The maximum speed exceeded 270 km per hour, with a phenomenal rate of acceleration, from 0 to 100 km per hour in 5.6 seconds, and 400 metres from a stationary start in 13.2 seconds. The ZR-1 is as fast as some other famous "supercars" such as the Ferrari Testarossa or the Porsche Carrera. There are faster cars around, like the F40 of the Lamborghini Diablo, but these are rather special cars and cost considerably more to buy.

LOLA.

COPERSUCAR.

Wings of every shape and size give competition vehicles a typical character.

FORMULA 1
FERRARI.

Sponsors
invade the
bodywork of
racing-cars.
The driver's
names on the
other hand
are almost
invisible.